A Fire in my Belly

poetry with a passion

A Fire in my Belly

poetry with a passion

Janet Piper

Coyote Creek Books | San José | California

ISBN-13: 978-1-946647-12-2

25 24 23 22 21 20 19 18 17   1 2 3 4 5 6 7

Published by Coyote Creek Books
www.coyotecreekbooks.com

It's the gift my daughter left me with
I am so very blessed to say
And with this gift
I make a wish
To be writing, everyday

To my son Joe, my grandson Xander, and my granddaughter Daphne.
Thank you for bringing so much joy into my life. I love you with all my heart!

Thanks mom
I love you

Belly on Fire

There's a fire in my belly!
I really love to write!
When I see a fascination
My thoughts, they do ignite!
I quickly grab a pad and pen
To jot down the poem that is in my head
If I don't take the time to write it down
The smile I had would soon be a frown
I want to please the people
To my readers I must cater!
If it's not quite right at the time
I can *always* change it later

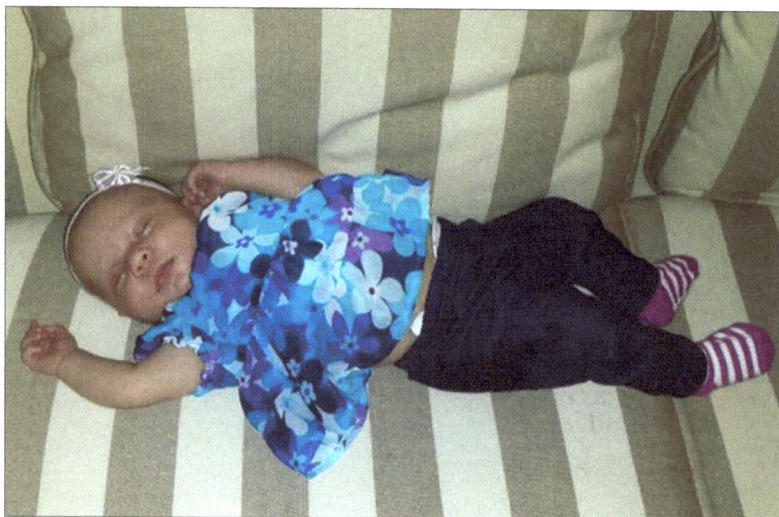

Happiness

This room is so cute and tasteful
It's wondrous to be here
I'm so much more than grateful
My happiness draws near

Morning Sounds

Do you ever wake up
To the sounds of birds chirping?
I'm happy to say that I do
They seem to be saying, "Good morning" to me
"I'm singing this song just for you"
Sometimes it's a little bit early to take
Sometimes they're right on queue
No need to set my alarm to awake
For the sounds of the morning
Are tried and true!

A Fire in my Belly

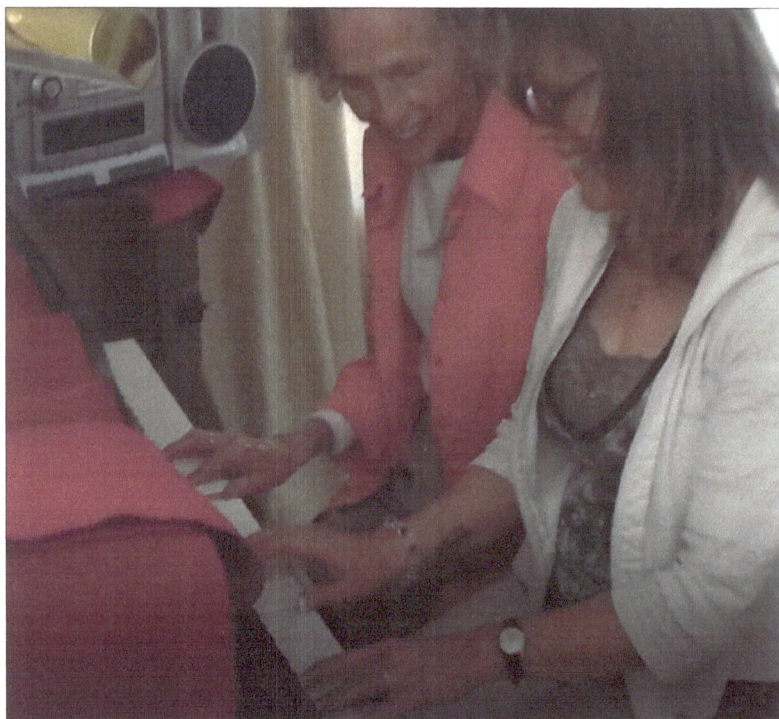

Piano Time

How I love to play the piano!
I wish I knew more songs
The black and white keys can't help but flow
And my yearning to learn just lingers on
I can sit and play for hours
Chopsticks are always fun
The pedals for your feet project with power
And I love it most, when I play with mom!

Fur Babies

Kittens and puppies
Become cats and dogs
We curl up with them on the couch
Or take take them out for morning jogs
They act just like our children
Some may even wear clothes
But we love our fur babies to the very end...
To the tip of each cold little nose!

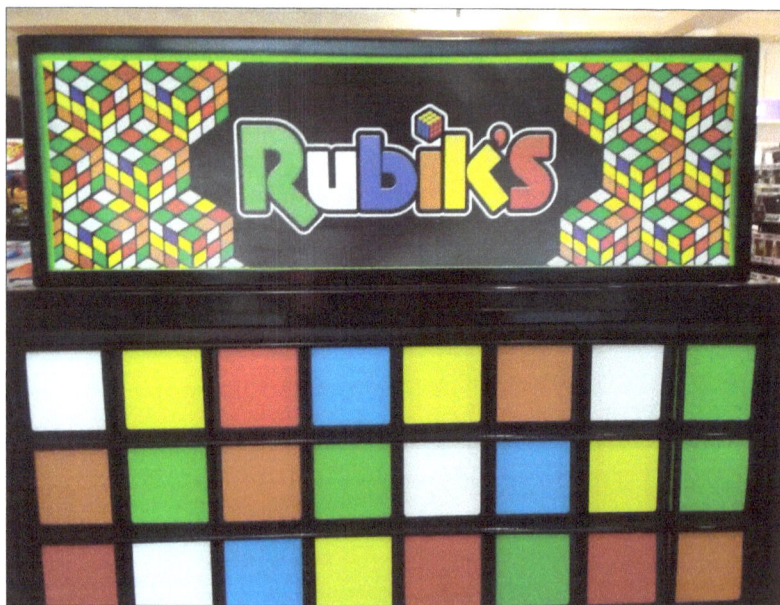

Rubik's Cube

Rubik's Cube
More bang for the buck
When I try to resolve
I just get stuck
But I won't give up without a fight
I'll twist it and turn it
'til I get it right!

Ellen

Ellen with pretty eyes of blue
She makes you smile
You know it's true
With Ellen you feel like a superstar!
No matter how near
Or even how far

The Key

The back door is locked
Someone has knocked
And I cannot find the key!
I look all around
From ceiling to ground
Thinking "Where in the world could it be?"
There's a meeting at eight
And we can't be late
The presentation must be grand!
I suddenly stop, for my eyes start to pop
At the key that is in my hand

A Fire in my Belly

Fireworks

We need to get right to the park
Or watch the cars fly by!
For the fun will start when it first gets dark
And adrenaline will run high
People coming with blankets and chairs
The place will fill up fast
Fireworks dancing in the air
Each more lovely than the last
So many pretty colors to see
We love the red white and blue
Smiles on all the faces, there be
And happiness when it's all through

Sisters
1989

My Sisters

I have two sisters that I dearly love
When it comes to family and friends
They always rise up and above
Whether it's cooking, baking, or cleaning
I just can't say enough
Even through the hardest times
We stay strong, and we stay tough
Although we may not always
Fit that perfect glove
I thank my lucky stars each night
To have my sisters I dearly love

A Fire in my Belly

In Canada

I'm surrounded by evergreen trees
That gracefully sway with each breeze
While visiting in Canada
I eat my cereal with banana
I can relax, take a walk
Or call home for a talk
And the peace puts my mind right at ease

Valentine

Valentine, you're in my heart
Although sometimes we seem miles apart
I look forward to the end of each day
When you walk through the door
And all I can say...
"I missed you my love, so very much
And just your hand, I need to touch..."

Thanksgiving

Banana Bread and Spice Cakes too
I'm so happy to spend
Thanksgiving with you!
I hope you enjoy your holiday feast
As I treasure our friendship
To say the least

Friends

Friends will come and friends will go
There are a few things about mine
That I'd like you to know
We're crazy about shopping
We take our leisurely lunches
But what's most important in our lives
Is we love each other... uh-bunches!!

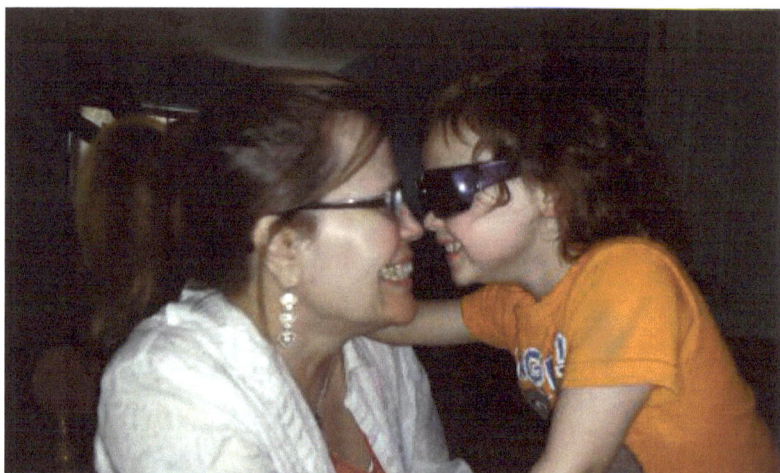

Life

There are lessons in life to be learned
So when you feel that the world has turned
Sit back, reflect, take a break, walk away
But don't stay gone for too many days
You'll find in your silence
You're not always in control
Look deep in your heart
And search your soul
See the good, and leave the rest
All you can do, is your very best
Each day you'll accomplish
Just a little bit more
For when true to yourself
Life opens a door!

My Brothers

So, you know about my sisters
But it stops, not even there
I just may have a brother or two
How many? Guess... I dare
It's more than five, but less than ten
Did you say nine? Nope, try again!
We're a little bit outnumbered
And they're always playing tricks
But we couldn't live without a one
So, I'll tell you now...
It's *seven*, not six!

Girl Talk

Dishes to wash and laundry to fold
Not that I mind
But it sometimes gets old
If I could just have an hour
To put my tired feet up
I'd love to join you for afternoon tea
Yes, please.. I'll take a cup
We can sit and chat about many things
The list goes on and on...
Or we can call the girls over
Act like we're teens
And talk about boys until dawn

Pacific Ocean

The Pacific Ocean, what a beautiful sight
I can stare at the water for hours on end
And pretend I'm a bird in flight
The ocean is calm when the sun's about
But when the tides roll in, you better watch out!
The waves will come crashing to beat the band
But when it's all said and done
You can play in the sand

Balance Rock

Balance Rock, how do you stand
On that tiny rock down below?
There must be something so great and so grand
To be still when the big winds blow

Movie Quotes

You'd remember these lines
Once you've heard
And my brothers can recite them
Word for word
They are from most movie quotes
Or maybe your favorite shows
Is everyone now all ready to play?
Let's see which one of us knows..
"I've got to have 30 minutes
Or the ship will blow apart!"
It's the show that has the best crew in it
And the Captain steals all the hearts
The plot would thicken halfway through
And within it, some kind of a wreck
You say you don't need another clue?
You've guessed it right...it's Star Trek!

Potato Skins

Potato Skins, Oh what a rush!
For my all-time favorite comfort food
They are an absolute must
I order them with extra cheese
And lots of bacon too
And with that, they're sure to please
With every mouth-watering chew
Whether dipping them in ranch sauce
Or just plain sour cream
They satisfy the craving in me
A potato skin lover's dream

A Fire in my Belly

Oranges

Is there a rhyme for orange?
I can't think of one
But I know they always catch my eye
When I see them sparkle
In the glistening sun
They are great to have with the morning meal
Or maybe an afternoon snack
Whatever the choice, and with each peel
It is hunger that I will lack
Oranges are so juicy and sweet
They give me so much might!
It is indeed a healthy, tasty treat
And I can never wait, to take a bite

Bowling

It's Tuesday night and I gotta 'roll'
I'm happy to say, it's time to bowl!
Getting a strike is the name of the game
But a pro, I can't say that I am
Although my average won't lead me to fame
My teammates still cheer when I get in a jam
The friends I see put a smile on my face
For life can take its toll
Each week I look forward to this happy place
And get all fired up, when it's time to bowl

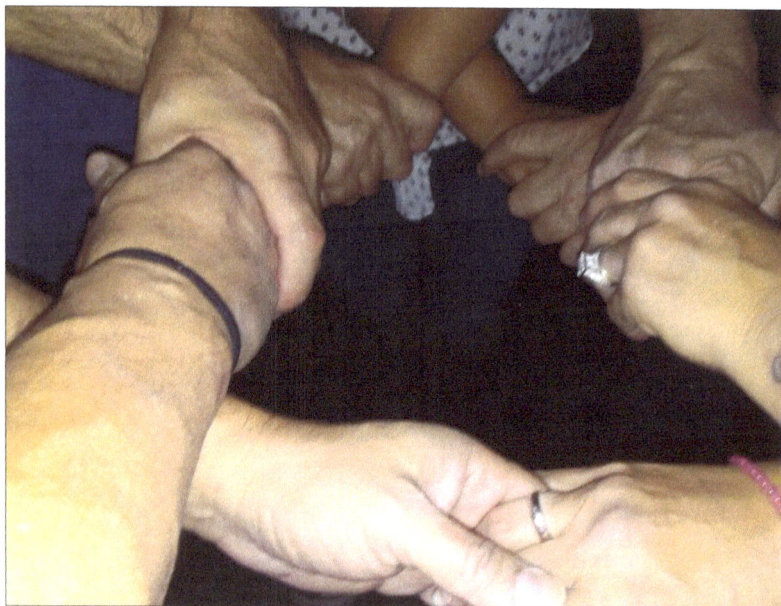

The Game

I'm remembering a game we played
When I was very young
Sometimes I'd be with the chosen few
Sometimes, not even one
We'd gather in a circle
Hold hands tight and say
"Tick tock, the game is locked
And nobody else can play
'Cuz if they do, I'll take off my shoe
And beat them black and blue!"
Of course the rules weren't written in stone
And before we knew it, no kid was alone

Fish Stories

Sitting on the boat
Waiting for a bite
This place is quite remote
We could be here all night
"I wish, I wish, I wish"
"I wish I had a fish!"
They say that wishes do come true
Let's see if it happens, in the big deep blue
What's this I see? I could be wrong?
Oh no I'm not! Hey look...FISH ON!
Six and a half pounds
Yet mighty tough
Did I catch him on my own?
Well maybe.....close enough!!

Journey Revisited

To Val, David, and Dave
To Kevin and to Frank
From the bottom of my heart
I do forever thank
The night I listened to you play
Was one of the best I've had so far
You turned my memories into song
And without a doubt, you raised the bar!
So anytime I'm feeling down
And my sadness needs relieving
I think of that special night in town
And hear those words
"Don't stop believing!"

Baby Girl

It's been six years since you went away
I love you and miss you, every day
Although my heart aches when I think of you
I know you're in Heaven, and you think of me, too
You're my little angel
You give everyone's heart a whirl
And all the people should know by now
You will always be
My baby girl

A Fire in my Belly

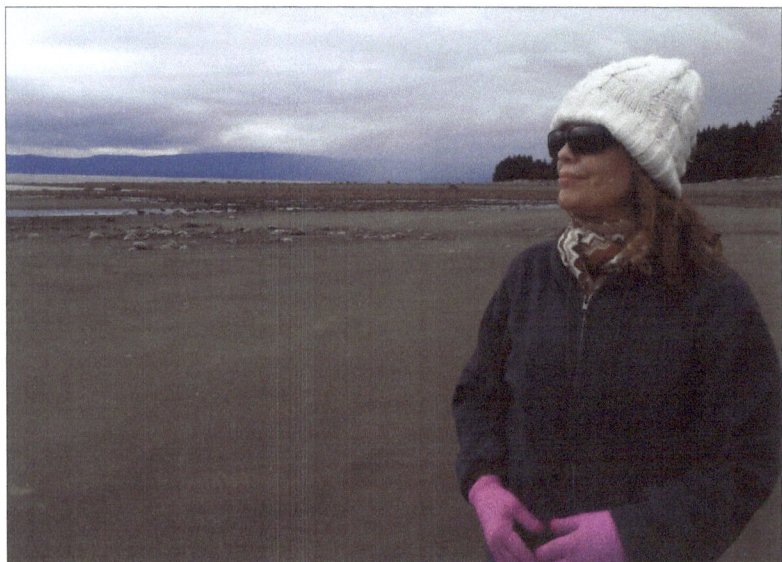

Timing

One minute you're on top
The next second you're not
It's all about the timing
If you wake up with a smile
Then your heart will go for miles
And it will all come out with the rhyming

Home

You're longing for adventure
An exciting sight unseen!
You pack your bags, destination unknown
Maybe Ireland, where it's all green
You conquer your fears and head down the road
With fascinations along the way
Exotic foods and pie ala mode
You think forever you're going to stay
But just a little reminder
Of mama's special home cooking
Will tug at your heart with tender thoughts
And soon a flight home you are booking
You've experienced new and unforgettable things
But with family in your heart, the love always rings
So, no matter the places you like to roam
Please make no mistake...
There's no place like home!

From the Heart

I write from the heart
I speak from the heart
My passion runs deep as the sea
Although from most readers I'm miles apart
My thanks for each one touches me

Acknowledgment

I would like to once again thank my family and friends for their support and contributions, during yet another exciting journey of publishing my second book.

I couldn't have done it without the love, strength, and encouragement from my amazing mother. She is my reason for being who I am today.

Thank you mom!

And to my publisher Jan McCutcheon, whom I wholeheartedly thank for her dedicated time, patience, and unwavering professionalism. I so much appreciate working with you, Jan.

www.ingramcontent.com/pod-product-compliance
Lightning Source LLC
Chambersburg PA
CBHW040036110426
42741CB00031B/109